Life's Journey

Erin Williams

BookLeaf Publishing

India | USA | UK

Life's Journey © 2024 Erin Williams

All rights reserved.

No part of this publication may be reproduced, stored in a retrieval system, or transmitted, in any form or by any means, electronic, mechanical, photocopying, recording or otherwise, without the prior written permission of the presenters.

Erin Williams asserts the moral right to be identified as author of this work.

Presentation by *BookLeaf Publishing*

Web: www.bookleafpub.com

E-mail: info@bookleafpub.com

ISBN: 9789360942182

First edition 2024

PREFACE

Poetry from the heart. I reflect on the beauty and pain of the world and our lives. I always try to find joy, even in dark times.

Never

Never say I love you,
If you really don't care.
Never talk about feelings,
Unless they are really there.
Never hold my hand,
If you're going to break my heart.
Never say you're going to,
Unless you plan to start.
Never look into my eyes,
If all you do is lie.
Never say hello,
If you meant goodbye.
If you really mean forever,
Then say you will try.
Never say forever,
Cause forever makes me cry.

Sleeping on the beach

Hold me in your arms this hot summer night.
All I want to feel is your warm embrace.
The waves singing a peaceful lullaby,
The sand soothing our skin and heat,
The stars lighting the way of our sweet dreams,
As we lay sleeping on the beach.
Our legs tangled together,
our skin tingling all over one another,
Our hearts beating as one,
As we lay sleeping on the beach.
The thunder rumbling above.
The lightening striking the water.
The waves crashing at our feet,
As I lay trembling in my sleep.
Now I'm all alone.
Drowning in a sea of depression,
Thinking of where he could be?
As I lay trembling in my sleep.
Suddenly jolted awake,
HIs concerned eyes gazing at me.
I sigh in relief.
It was only a dream sleeping on the beach.
Falling asleep again to the peaceful waves,
Letting the same cool our skin,
Tangling up in each other's love,

As we lay sleeping on the beach.
Hold me in your arms this hot summer night,
All I need to feel is your warm embrace.

No More

No more sad poems,
No more tears.
I finally succeeded,
Without any fear.
No more misery,
No more sorrow,
I live for happiness,
No longer for tomorrow.
Today could be it,
You'll never know.
So live while you can,
And move very slow.
Enjoy every creature,
Enjoy every moment,
Don't let days pass by,
Without a second glance.
Because once you're gone,
There is no other chance.
Find someone you love,
Give them a hug and kiss.
If they're gone tomorrow,
You won't know what you missed.
Live and be happy,
While you're still on Earth.
End will come soon,

and Prove it's worth.
The point to this poem
Is to warn everyone,
That today may be your last
Before all is done.

Cabin

There's a cabin deep within.
No one should go near it; it's filled with sin.
For miles and miles there are fences around,
No one can get in, no one's allowed.
It's a mystery to some,
And very few people were ever welcome.
Those that use to come and stay,
Broke the only rule.
Causing it to lock up its doors,
And turn itself cruel.
There's a cabin deep inside,
Lots of things stay there and hide.
It lets no one through its gates of steel,
For its afraid someone will start up its wheel.

Crushes

Crushes come and go,
Lovers always leave.
Hearts get broken,
Wounds never heal.
But one thing I know,
Is that true friends always last.

Alone

I had them both,
Close as can be.
Then one after another,
They slipped away from me.
I loved them both,
But in different ways.
And yet they were far from me,
Gone within days.
It started with him,
that so-called friend,
When he turned his back on me.
And before I knew it,
My one true love to be,
Joined him and became my enemy.
I lost them both,
And even though they may have lost me,
At least they have each other.
And me? What about me?
Waiting for another?
Another what? Heartbreak?
I am left alone.

Desire

There is a desire,
It's more than a want,
Less than a need.
We all have it inside,
When it comes, we'll never know.
How long it lasts,
Cannot be answered.
There is a desire,
It's deep down inside,
It's worse than a hunger,
More profound than knowledge.
What is this desire?
It's Love.

You

At first glance I never would have guessed
that I would end up feeling this way.
I found you attractive,
I fell for your charm,
and even though I knew better,
I fell into your arms.
Every time I see you,
my face lights up.
And even worse my heart begins to soar;
because I know that no matter what everyone
says,
I want to love you even more.
When you make me mad,
I can't help but laugh.
But when you make me sad,
I can't help but cry.
I want to understand you,
but you refuse to open up.
I know you've been hurt in the past,
So have I.
But if you could learn to trust me,
and open your heart,
You would finally see,
that all I want from you
is to be with me.

Stuck

It seems to me that you're still in my mind.
I thought I could forget you,
but that didn't get me far.
I can't deny my love for you,
and that I really do miss you too.
I would have done anything for you,
even given you unconditional love.
Instead I'm sitting here lonely,
always in a bad mood,
cause without your love
my hearts not complete.
And how can I live without a full beat?
I beg myself, Please forget him,
but my heart won't listen.
My friends say to move on,
but I can't listen to them.
I'm lost without you, can't you see?
And if I could only have one more chance,
We would fit together I promise you;
and all our worries would be one,
and then together we could move on.

Too Young

I don't know what to do,
because all I can think about is you.
You say I'm too young and would only change
my mind,
But how do you know if you won't give it a try.
What harm could it do if you opened up your
heart,
and let me in, no more than now.
you can't see the hurt you cause me,
You can't feel the pain,
But I know you wouldn't regret it,
because of the love we could share.
I might be young, out of reach, "indecisive," or
whatever else it is,
but like once said in a movie,
"I am just a girl standing in front of a boy,
asking him to love her"
Don't you feel this too?
You can't lie and say it isn't true.
Why are you putting me through this, even you?
It must be those people at work, the ones that are
so persistent..
But, please whatever you do, don't turn away
because of someone else
It's happened before and it's worse than any
heartbreak in the world.

A Poem for You Know Who

He stands so near to me, I can feel his heart beat
He seems so close to me, but he's too far away to
touch
This figure before me is so desired
Yet very hard to get
I reach and reach and yearn to touch him
But all I feel is the cold air between us
This young, irresistible figure keeps standing
there,
knowing that I keep reaching for him,
but all he does is step further away
He's treating me, my heart, my love like a virus,
as if he touches me, it'll get a hold of him
Like I'm a disease that will engulf his soul
and just tear it apart, until nothing is left
He knows the effect he has on me,
but he does nothing
To protect himself, he encloses his heart in
isolation
puts a barricade around it, allowing no one to
pass
Yet, I continue to reach for this figure,
hoping one day the air will warm between us
And I can pass through all of the blocks
And truly touch his heart.

Soulmate

Meeting from a distance was a sign of our
destiny.
For once everything is falling right into place.
The first time I talked to you,
I knew I felt something that had never been there
before.
There was a deep connection that I know we
both felt,
but feared to say it.
Even though we hadn't met,
I knew it was our destiny, our fate.
I had always dreamed about a feeling like this,
Hoping some day, I would know my soulmate.,
Now I know what it's like to know you're with
the one
After only a few days I knew I wanted to be with
only you.
I was ready to give myself completely;
My mind, body, heart and soul belonged to you.
Then, finding you had the same feelings put all
the pieces together
Every second I talk to you,
Takes away a tear I've cried in the past.
Being with you for one moment was worth all
the pain I had to go through,

It never would have come together
If the past had been changed in any way.
What's even funnier is that I'm writing these
words before we had our first meeting,
That's how I know it's all real
I like you, I love you, I'm in love with you.
I want to be the perfect wife for you,
And I will do this for the rest of my life.

Vows

Someone I can just be me around
Someone that is always on my mind
Somone who makes my heart beat faster and
slower at the same time
Somone who shares my hopes and dreams in life
Someone who holds the same unconditional love
for me
Somone who is only perfect in my eyes
Somone who sees the best and worst in me, but
still loves me
Somone I can talk to for hours and never say a
word
Someone who listens to me and hears everything
I say
Someone who is my best friend, companion and
love
Someone who knows how I'm feeling without
really asking
Somone I can always be around and still have
plenty of space
Someone who knows it's the little things that
count the most
Someone that completes me so I won't need
anyone else
Someone I have to be with in order to truly live

Someone who makes me feel that home is
wherever they are
Someone who can always make me laugh even
when I'm crying
Someone whose worth everything even if it's
only for one moment alone
Someone that doesn't care what others thing, as
long as we're together
Someone would wouldn't take one second
together for granted
Somone who is part of me, my life, my love, my
soul
Someone like you

Escape

Trapped in an unknown story
Wondering where this life is going
Do I take the journey without question
Do I try to escape and be on my own
Feeling the worry and fear of others
Makes me question every single turn we take
Shall I stay here and wait for my fate
Or do I take the leap and try to escape
The journey is drawing near to the end
I know I need to make a choice soon, but what
to do
What of everyone else, do they feel the same?
Should I wait to see what they choose
Follow the herd, stay with the pack, like a clone
Or do I take the plunge and risk being alone
Will the world accept my choice and let me be
Or will I be forced back on the same journey
Instincts kick in and I know what must be done
As I leap and plunge all I can think of is bathing
in the sun
Someone saw what I did and came to rescue me
I just hope that all of us will one day be set free

Circles

Work, money, bills, repeat
How do we live with so much heat
Why is our world consumed with material things
Enjoy each day, live your life, you say
But how when the world is run by money
Work, work, work, money, bills, bills, bills
No time left to travel or be fulfilled
Dreams become distant regrets
Wrinkles, gray hairs, old age sets in
Is it too late to live now or just begin
Now I'm at the end
Why did I work so much, let bills and things
consume me
Memories are a distant dream
At least all my bills were paid and I had things
The pictures faded with my youth
Please turn back the time, I will do it right
Cherish little things, experience everything in
sight
You only live once, that is Wrong!
You live every day, we only die once
So live every day
Take advantage of life every day
Before age creeps up on you and you can no
longer play

Zen

Salty breeze blows through my hair
Falling into the embrace of the warm sun
Wet, soft grains of sand surrond my feet
As they sink in deeper, becoming one with the
beach
Waves crashing with my every heart beat
Wishing I could say away into your abyss
Always right where I left you
Singing through the breeze, crashing against the
sand
You bring me inner peace, calming me, washing
away every worry with each wave
The shells you leave are tiny memories
Reminding me, you are always there
Full of mystery and beauty, I hope to explore the
depts of your wonder
ONce past the rough surface, there is serenity
surrounding me
You are soothing, flowing to your own beat
Now I know why you are like a magnet to me

Enough

It's okay to be struggling and feel lost
You can still be happy and rejoice
Everything may not be going your way
But it doesn't mean one thing in your life can
define you
What ha you down; love, money, loss?
Find joy and peace in something else each day
Work through the grief that you feel
You can still be significant for yourself
You can still be worthy
You are significant; You are worthy
Don't let anyone or anything take away your
value
Finding joy amongst the chaos is a true treasure
Life throws lessons at us in many ways
Embrace it, acknowledge the struggle, and move
on

Innocence

So many people look at you in fear
Juding you without a second glance
Even when your sweet and loving demeanor is
clear
All you want is a loving place to call home
with some treats, a bed, toys, and belly rubs
And a person that loves you unconditionally to
call your own
You wonder why people have so much hate
And how their ignorance can decide your fate
If only you could talk and tell them how much
love you have
Tell them you want to protect them with love
Tell them your size doesn't define you
Ask them to just give you a chance at life
Maybe then they won't believe the stereotypes
Maybe they will stop listening to all the hype
Look into your eyes and really see you
Understand that what they say isn't true
Stop taking your life and freedom, because they
choose to believe what others say
We will continue to fight for your lives every
day
There are good people that know your true heart
Some just don't know where to start

Keep your innocence and happy wiggles going
strong
We will work together to prove everyone else
wrong

Rain

Feeling the temperature change slightly with
anticipation of your arrival
Fresh smell in the air as the clouds come over
the sky
Cold and wet tiny pellets begin to come down,
feeding the Earth
So much beauty comes from such a simple drop
So much destruction can come from the same
drop
Cleanse everything, refresh the ground, wash
away the evil.
Create a playground for the innocent at heart.
Whatever your purpose for the day, I enjoy the
pleasures you bring to the senses.